Charles Francis Adams

# An Address on the Life, Character and Services of William Henry Seward

Delivered at the Request of Both Houses of the Legislature of New York, at

Albany, April 18, 1873

.

Charles Francis Adams

**An Address on the Life, Character and Services of William Henry Seward**
*Delivered at the Request of Both Houses of the Legislature of New York, at Albany, April 18, 1873*

ISBN/EAN: 9783744711623

Printed in Europe, USA, Canada, Australia, Japan

Cover: Foto ©ninafisch / pixelio.de

More available books at **www.hansebooks.com**

# AN ADDRESS

ON THE

## Life, Character and Services

OF

# WILLIAM HENRY SEWARD.

DELIVERED

At the Request of both Houses of the Legislature of New York,
At Albany, April 18, 1873,

BY

## CHARLES FRANCIS ADAMS.

———

ALBANY:
WEED, PARSONS AND COMPANY.
1873.

# In Memoriam.

---

## PROCEEDINGS

#### OF THE

## Legislature of the State of New York

#### ON THE DEATH OF

## Ex-Governor William H. Seward.

---

### State of New York:

#### IN SENATE,

##### JANUARY 22, 1873.

On motion of Mr. PERRY:

RESOLVED, That a select committee of three be appointed, on the part of the Senate, to meet with a committee on the part of the Assembly, to report resolutions expressive of the sense of the Legislature, relative to the decease of ex-Governor WILLIAM H. SEWARD, and that, if the Assembly concur therein, the Senate will meet at 12 o'clock noon, on Friday, the 24th instant, for hearing the report of said committee.

The President appointed as such committee, on the part of the Senate, Senators PERRY, WOODIN and JOHNSON.

IN ASSEMBLY,

JANUARY 23, 1873.

RESOLVED, That the Assembly do concur in the resolution adopted by the Senate, relative to the death of ex-Governor SEWARD; and that Messrs. CLAPP, VAN COTT, BLACKIE, BEEBE and MCGUIRE be appointed as such committee on the part of the Assembly.

The joint committee, to which the subject was referred, reported the following preamble and resolutions, which were unanimously adopted :

WHEREAS, after the adjournment of the Legislature, at its last session, the country heard, with the deepest sorrow, of the death of WILLIAM H. SEWARD, ex-Governor of the State of New York ; therefore,

*Resolved*, That the Legislature of the State of New York is profoundly sensible of the great loss which the State and the Nation have thus sustained.

*Resolved*, That while we lament such loss, we still experience a mournful satisfaction and a lofty pride in recalling the varied and invaluable services which he rendered to his country; the acknowledged ability and patriotic zeal with which he, on all occasions, maintained her rights and defended her honor; the purity of his character, the grandeur of his intellectual endowments, the variety and extent of his learning, and the industry, fearlessness and fidelity which ever marked his career, both in public and private life.

*Resolved*, That the Legislature of this State tender to the family of the deceased its sincere condolence upon the sad bereavement which has removed from the domestic circle its affectionate and illustrious head.

*Resolved,* That the joint committee be and they hereby are authorized and requested to make such arrangements as they may deem proper for the commemoration of the solemn event, by the delivery of an oration before the two Houses by some distinguished citizen.

*Resolved,* That, as a testimony of respect, the two Houses of the Legislature do now adjourn.

*Committee on part of the Senate :*

JOHN C. PERRY,
WM. B. WOODIN
WM. JOHNSON,

*Committee on part of the Assembly :*

W. S. CLAPP,
GEO. M. BEEBE,
CHAS. BLACKIE,
DAVID C. VAN COTT,
J. McGUIRE.

In pursuance of the foregoing resolutions, the joint committee reported that they had tendered to the Hon. CHARLES FRANCIS ADAMS an invitation to deliver the memorial address, and that he had accepted the invitation.

The following is the correspondence :

# LEGISLATIVE PROCEEDINGS.

## LETTER TO MR. ADAMS.

### "STATE OF NEW YORK:

"SENATE CHAMBER,
"ALBANY, *February* 8, 1873.

" Hon. CHARLES FRANCIS ADAMS:

" *Dear Sir* — I have the honor herewith to transmit an authenticated copy of the report of a select committee of our State Legislature, who were appointed under a concurrent resolution of the Senate and Assembly, ' to report resolutions, etc., expressive of the sense of the Legislature relative to the decease of ex-Governor WILLIAM H. SEWARD,' which report has been unanimously adopted.

" At a meeting of the two committees, held pursuant to the resolution contained in the report, it was unanimously resolved to invite you to deliver an address at some convenient time during the session, suitable to the occasion; and the undersigned chairman of the joint committee was instructed to communicate such invitation.

" Aside from other considerations, the committee, in tendering this invitation, beg leave to state that, inasmuch as the deceased, on the occasion of the death of your honored father, delivered an oration to his memory before our State Legislature, the committee feel that nothing could be more appropriate, and nothing afford the friends of the honored dead a greater degree of satisfaction than to have you, on this interesting and solemn occasion, reciprocate the favor by accepting this invitation.

" Requesting the favor of an early reply,

" I am,

" Yours, very respectfully,

" JOHN C. PERRY,

" *Chairman of Joint Committee.*"

## MR. ADAMS' REPLY.

" 57 MOUNT VERNON STREET,
" BOSTON, *February* 12, 1873.

" Hon. J. C. PERRY,

" *Chairman, etc., Senate of New York, Albany:*

" *Dear Sir* — I have to acknowledge the reception, this morning, of your letter of the 8th instant, and of a copy of the resolutions adopted by the Legislature of New York, on the occasion of the decease of their eminent statesman, the late W. H. SEWARD.

" On behalf of the joint committee authorized to act under one of those resolutions, you, as their chairman, have been pleased to signify to me their wish that I should deliver the address contemplated.

" Profoundly sensible of the honor conferred upon me, I feel as if I could not decline the task, however unworthy to perform it.

" In accepting it, however, it becomes of some importance to me to know what period of time can be allotted to me within which to accomplish the work. As much of the material which I should wish to gather for the purpose must be found scattered

4

far and wide, and the sessions of the Legislature are already considerably advanced, this becomes a question upon which my absolute decision must turn. I should be sorry to do a hurried or hasty thing upon so great an occasion.

" I am, very truly,

" Your obedient servant,

" CHARLES FRANCIS ADAMS."

### Second Letter to Mr. Adams.

" STATE OF NEW YORK :

" Senate Chamber,
" Albany, *February* 13, 1873.

" Hon. Charles Francis Adams,
*Boston, Mass. :*

" *Dear Sir* — Your letter of the 12th accepting the invitation contained in my communication of the 8th instant, to deliver an address on the late William H. Seward, before the New York Legislature, was received this morning, and laid before the joint committee.

" In reply, I beg leave to state that the committee have instructed me to tender their very sincere thanks for your prompt and cordial acceptance of their invitation, and to inform you that it is their opinion that the session of the Legislature will not terminate before the 20th of April.

" The committee, therefore, will set apart for the memorial occasion any day prior to that time, which you may be pleased to designate.

" Very respectfully and obediently yours,

"JOHN C. PERRY,

" *Chairman of Joint Committee.*"

The day finally fixed upon for the memorial proceedings was Friday, the 18th day of April — the exercises to be held in the North Reformed Church.

On the day designated, the Legislature and invited guests assembled at the Capitol, and, headed by his Excellency, Governor John A. Dix, and staff, proceeded in a body to the church, where the following exercises took place, his Excellency presiding, assisted by Lieutenant-Governor John C. Robinson, President of the Senate, and the Hon. A. B. Cornell, Speaker of the Assembly.

# Exercises at the Church.

ORGAN. — INTRODUCTORY.

QUARTETTE. — "How Sleep the Brave," - Rooke.
Arranged by J. R. Thomas.

PRAYER. — By Rev. Rufus W. Clark, D. D.

Almighty Father, we adore Thee as the Sovereign of the Universe, the source of our being, and the arbiter of our destiny. We worship Thee as our King, and render thanks to Thee for all the advantages and blessings of life. We realize our entire dependence upon Thee, for every faculty of our nature, and gifts of Thy providence; and we seek Thy guidance in our daily duties. We thank Thee for the gifts of Thy Son, who brought with Him to earth, a heart that beat in sympathy with every form of human sorrow. We rejoice, that standing at the grave, He announced Himself as the Resurrection and the Life, to all who believe. May we have faith in Him, and in the power and fruits of the Resurrection. May Thy Holy Spirit descend and rest upon this vast assemblage; illuminating every heart, and making of every soul a temple of the living God. Do Thou guide in the services of this interesting and solemn occasion. While we mourn the departure of Thy servant, whose death has summoned us here to-day, we sorrow not as those who have no hope. We thank Thee for His pure and elevated character; for the rigid integrity associated with his eminent natural abilities; for his devotion to human rights, and the force and eloquence with which he defended them. We

7

bless Thee for his noble contributions to the cause of national liberty, and that in the conflict which his prophetic eye saw was "irrepressible," he was always found on the side of justice, humanity, and God. Standing on the platform of human rights and civil freedom, he publicly declared that if necessary, he would stand alone; and we thank Thee that Thou didst stand with him, to sustain him. We are grateful to Thee for his reverence for religion; for his faith in the Lord Jesus Christ as his Saviour; for his interest in the church, in Christian education, and in all enterprises that contribute to the extension of the Redeemer's Kingdom. We thank Thee that Thou didst comfort him in his last hours, and that the hope of immortality dawned upon his spirit, as he departed from earth to Heaven.

We commend to Thee the bereaved relatives and friends, beseeching Thee that they may ever trust in Thee, and exercise that faith in Christ, that will secure a reunion with the departed, in the realms of the blessed.

We invoke Thy blessing upon all gathered here to-day, that Thou wouldst aid them in the faithful discharge of the duties of their several spheres. Grant that our rulers may be enriched with divine grace, inspired with pure patriotism, and be qualified to administer government for the best good of the people and the honor of God. Bless Thy servant, the President of the United States, and those associated with him in authority; our national Senators and Representatives, and all holding positions of public responsibility and trust. May our Government reflect the principles of Thy divine government, that law and justice may be maintained, liberty preserved, and the prosperity of the nation secured. Bless Thy servant, the Governor of this Commonwealth, and those connected with him in the administration of public affairs. We render thanks to Thee for their disposition and ability to maintain the laws against crime; and that while they would gladly extend mercy to the penitent, they have revealed the strength of the Government to protect the property, rights and lives of its loyal citizens.

Let Thy blessing rest upon our State Senators and Representatives, that they may be inspired with the principles of integrity and a pure, lofty patriotism. May all realize that any advantage or gain, secured by the sacrifice of principle, ceases to be an advantage. May they possess the wealth of conscious uprightness, and the satisfaction of having faithfully met and discharged every duty.

Bless Thy servant, providentially called to address us to-day. We thank Thee for his sympathy with the principles and character of the illustrious dead, and for his eminent services rendered to the Nation. We bless Thee that, while enabled to secure the rights of the American people, he aided in promoting peace between two nations bound together by the same language and religion, and by mutual desires to advance civilization, and extend the Kingdom of our Lord Jesus Christ.

We pray for Thy richest blessings to descend upon the American Republic. We thank Thee for our free institutions; our pure religion; our system of popular education; our social and domestic advantages, and the prosperity we have received from Thee. Thou didst preserve the ship of State in the tempest that threatened her destruction, and we pray that divine wisdom may continue to guide us, and Almighty Power continue to bless us.

And now we seek preparation to follow our departed friend, whose virtues and services we are assembled to commemorate. Help us so to live that death may be life.

May the music of angelic hosts and songs of the redeemed welcome us to the Heavenly home. May we gaze with delight upon celestial cities, and temples of divine beauty, and meeting in the city of God, with a great multitude that no man can number, we will ascribe blessing and honor and glory and power unto Him that sitteth upon the throne, and unto the Lamb, forever and ever. AMEN.

*ORGAN SOLO.* — " Dead March in Saul,"  -  *Handel.*

*READING of the Memorial Resolutions of the Legislature.* By CHARLES R. DAYTON, CLERK OF THE SENATE.

*RECITATIVE and ARIA.* —" The Trumpet shall Souud." *Handel.*  J. R. THOMAS.

*INTRODUCTION OF THE ORATOR.* By Gov. JOHN A. DIX, as follows :

A quarter of a century ago, this very month, and within these walls, WILLIAM H. SEWARD delivered a memorial discourse on the character and public services of John Quincy Adams. And to-day the son of Mr. Adams is here to pronounce a similar discourse on Mr. Seward. Thus, with these two kindred ceremonies are associated the names of three eminent statesmen, who have shared largely in the confidence and respect of their countrymen, and who, by their distinguished talents and the purity of their lives, have contributed as largely to their country's welfare and reputation. I present to you the Hon. CHARLES FRANCIS ADAMS.

*THE HON. CHARLES FRANCIS ADAMS then delivered the following Address :*

10

# THE ADDRESS.

———

FELLOW-CITIZENS OF THE SENATE AND ASSEMBLY
OF NEW YORK:

You have honored me by an invitation to perform
a duty, from the difficulty of which I shrink, the
closer I approach it. I undertake it only with an
assurance that, were my powers equal to my will, I
should erect a monument more durable than marble
or brass.

The subject is fascinating, from the wide views
which it opens of the noblest career of human life,
and the highest aspirations of mortal ambition.
Whatever may be the value of the modern speculations touching the origin of man, it seems quite clear
that his intellectual stature has not essentially
changed since the era when we find, in Greece, the
most difficult social problems discussed with a pro-
foundness never since surpassed. It is in one of the
familiar dialogues reported by the philosopher Plato
as having been held by Socrates, with his disciples,
that the question is gravely presented whether such

11

a union be possible, in one and the same individual, as that of a philosopher and a statesman. What this combination means is admirably rendered by the latest translator in these words: "A man in whom the power of thought and action is perfectly balanced, equal to the present, reaching forward to the future." The conclusion drawn from that conversation was that such a person, ruling in a constitutional state, had not yet been seen. More than two thousand years have elapsed since this testimony was recorded, and the solution of the problem, with the added experience of an historic record, embracing the lives of sixty generations of the race, far more widely observed over the globe, is still to seek.

### HAS THERE EVER BEEN SUCH A MAN.

Without attempting to enter upon such a topic, demanding a life-time of research, it may, perhaps, be permitted to me to observe that, from what we may learn of the career of all those who have since been competitors in this noblest of human pursuits, it is possible for us to deduce some general laws of human action valuable to bear in mind. Praying your pardon for my boldness, I would, then, venture to suggest that, by a comparison of the multitude of examples, we may readily reduce them all to a classi-fication consisting of three forms.

The first and lowest of these embraces all those

lives in which power has been exercised mainly for personal ends, with little regard to the public good. If called to give an example of this class, I should name the noted Cleon, of Athens, as delineated so forcibly by his contemporaries, Thucydides, the historian, and Aristophanes, the dramatist. But this type of a public man, called a demagogue in a democracy, does not change its essence by transfer to more absolute forms of government. The interested flatterer of the people simply puts on a laced coat and becomes the courtier of a monarch or any other sovereign power, one or many. Cleon, stimulating the passions of the Athenians to the massacre of the male population of Mitylene, was only working for his own influence, just as Ashley Cooper, Lord Shaftesbury, stimulating the treacherous policy of the Second Charles in Great Britain,

"The pillars of the public safety shook ,"

and just as Manuel Godoy, the Prince of Peace, by his selfish counsels precipitated the fall of the pitiful Charles of Spain.

This, then, is the class which works the injury of nations.

The next, and second division, includes those who with pure motives and equal capacity address themselves to the work of maintaining the existing state of things as it is. Their aim is to reënforce established ideas, and confirm ancient institutions. Of this type I would specify as examples, Cicero in antiquity, Sir Robert Walpole, Cardinal Mazarin, Prince Kaunitz, in later times.

2. This is the class which sustains nations.

The third and last division consists of those who, possessing a creative force, labor to advance the condition of their fellow-men. Of such I find a type in Pericles, in Gregory I, and in Cardinal Richelieu.

3. This is the class which develops nations.

Measuring the life of WILLIAM HENRY SEWARD by this scale, I have no scruple in enrolling his name in the third and highest class. In my mind his case bears analogy to that of Pericles,* with this difference, that the sphere of his action was one by the side of which that of the other dwindles into nothing.

On this occasion it is not my design to follow the common course of a purely chronological narrative. It would absorb too much time; besides which, that work has been already well done by others who have preceded me. It will suffice to state that Mr. Seward was born with the century, and issued from the college at Schenectady at the age of nineteen. Three years passed in the customary probation of a lawyer's office gave him his profession, and one year

---

* Any reader curious to know more of the grounds for this opinion is referred to the character given of this statesman by Grote. History of Greece, volume v, pp. 435–9.

more found him married. In the words of the
sagacious Lord of Verulam, he had "given hostages
to fortune," and very early "assumed impediments to
great enterprises, whether of virtue or mischief."
From that moment he could hope to enlarge the
basis of his imperfect education only by snatching
what he might out of the intervals of rest in a busy life.
Hence it becomes proper to assume that, in the just
sense of the word, Mr. Seward was never a learned
man. In the ardor with which he rushed into affairs,
the wonder is that he acquired what he did. To his
faculty of rapid digestion of what he could read, he
was indebted for the attainments he actually mastered.

For it should be further remarked that, though
he faithfully applied himself to his profession, it was
not an occupation congenial to his taste. On the
contrary, he held it in aversion. He felt in himself
a capacity to play a noble part on the more spacious
theater of State affairs. His aspiration was for the
fame of a statesman, and, in indulging this propensity,
he committed no mistake.

The chief characteristic of his mind was its breadth
of view. In this sense he was a philosopher study-
ing politics. He began by forming for himself a
general idea of government, by which all questions
of a practical nature that came up for consideration
were to be tested. This naturally led him to prefer
the field of legislation to that of administration,

though he proved equally skillful in both. Almost simultaneously with his marriage, he appeared ready to launch into the political conflicts of the hour. Commencing in his small way, he rose by easy degrees into the atmosphere of statesmanship. I distinguish between these conditions, not to derogate from either. In our past experience there have been many politicians who have not become statesmen. So, also, there have been many statesmen who were never politicians. Mr. Seward was equally at home in both positions.

But, inasmuch as this made up the true career which he followed, I am driven to the necessity of considering it almost exclusively. And, while so doing, I am also constrained to plunge more or less deeply into the Serbonian bog of obsolete party politics. I am not insensible to the nature of the difficulties under which I labor in an exposition of this kind. On the one side I run a risk of trying your patience by tedious reference to stale excitements; and on the other, of raking over the ashes of fires still holding heat enough to burn. All I can say in excuse is that, in my belief, no correct delineation of the course of this eminent leader can be made without it. Permit me only to add a promise that, in whatever I feel it my duty to say, it will be my endeavor to be guided by as calm and impartial a spirit as the lot of humanity will admit. Happily, my purpose is facilitated at this moment, by the fact that the passions which so fiercely raged during the period I am to review are in a measure laid asleep by the removal of the chief causes which set them in motion.

The political history of the country under its present form of government naturally divides itself into two periods of nearly equal length. The first embraces the administration of the first five presidents, and the settlement of the principles upon which a policy was guided, as well at home as abroad. But by reason of the almost continuous embarrassments occasioned by the violent conflicts then raging over the entire Continent of Europe, the agitation of parties had its chief source in conflicting views of foreign rather than domestic questions. Hence it came to a natural end with the reëstablishment of a general peace. The foundation of parties having failed, there followed an interval of harmony, which, at the time, was known by the name of the " era of good feelings."

Suddenly there sprang up a contest, wholly new in its nature, the first sound of which the veteran Jefferson, in his retreat at Monticello, likened to that of a fire-bell at night. The territory of Missouri wished to be organized, and admitted into the Union as a State. An effort was made to affix a condition that negro slavery should not be permitted there.

The line of division between the free and the slave-holding States was at once defined, and, for a time, the battle was fought in the halls of Congress with the greatest pertinacity. With equal suddenness the quarrel was appeased by the adoption of a proposal denominated "a compromise," and matters seemed again to settle down in the old way.

The general election for the presidency followed. The evidence of the complete disorganization of parties was made visible in the multiplication of the candidates. Five aspirants were brought forward by their respective friends, four out of the five from the slave-holding States. In this state of distraction, it was not unnatural that the single candidate from the free States should have an advantage. He was elected.

But four years later appeared a very different state of things. The slave-holding States had then concentrated on their most popular candidate, and, forming an alliance with a large section of the popular party in the North, they effected a complete establishment of their power. Here is the origin of the division of parties which prevailed for more than thirty years. But it should be noted that this was predicated upon the basis of what was called "the compromise" established by the Missouri question, and a consequent tacit understanding that the subject of negro slavery was to be as much excluded from political discussion as if it did not exist.

The great State of New York had, by a division of its electoral votes, contributed little or nothing to the triumph. But, after the decisive result, an organization followed, which, by pledging itself to the fortunes of the new dynasty, succeeded in maintaining its ascendency for many years. This claimed to be the popular, or Democratic, party. In opposition were soon arrayed the class, in the free States, leaning to conservative opinions in all questions connected with the security of property; and with them were combined under the leadership of an eminent statesman of the West, Henry Clay, so much of the population of that section as could be attracted to his banner. This was finally known as the Whig party. It follows from this statement that the issues made between these parties were mainly confined to superficial questions of management of the public affairs or the construction of Federal powers. Hence it happened, singularly enough, that, for a considerable period of time, the disputes were turned in a direction which had no reference whatever to the most serious part of the policy upon which the Government was secretly acting. That policy was the extension of the slave-holding power by gaining new territory over which to spread it.

For it should be observed that, while a profound silence was observed at home, the new Administration had not been long settled in its place, before secret agencies were set in motion, through the diplomatic department, to procure expansion in the direction in which this object could be the most easily effected. This pointed southwest to Texas, a territory then forming a part of the Mexican Republic.

Such being the state of things at the outset of Mr. Seward's career, the first thing necessary for him to do was to choose his side. Under his father's roof the influences naturally carried him to sympathize with the old Jeffersonian party on the one hand, while the relics of the slave-system remaining in the family as house-servants, the least repulsive form of that relation, seemed little likely to inspire in him much aversion to it on the other. Nevertheless, he early formed his conclusions adversely to the organization in New York professing to be the successors of the Jefferson school, and not less so to the perpetuation of slavery anywhere. The reason for this is obvious. With his keen perception of the operation of general principles, he penetrated at once the fact that the resurrection, in this form, of the old party was not only hollow, but selfish. It looked to him somewhat like a close corporation, made for the purpose of dealing in popular doctrines, not so much for the public benefit as for that of the individual directors. Moreover, it became clear that, among those doctrines, that of freedom to the slave was rigorously excluded by reason of the bond of union entered into with his masters at the South. In reality, he was, in principle, too democratic for the Democrats. Hence, he waged incessant war against this form of oligarchy down to the hour when it was finally broken up.

On the other hand, the selection of the more conservative side, which he finally made, was one not unattended with difficulty. The idea of a popular form of government which he had built up in his own mind was one of the most expansive kind. He applied it to our system, and saw at once the means of its development almost indefinitely. In the variety of details as they passed before him, whether it was legislation, education, immigration, internal or external communication, personal or religious liberty, social equalization, or national expansion, he viewed the treatment of all in his large, generalizing way, always subject, however, to the regulation of general laws. In this he was conservative, that he sought to change, only the better to expand on a wider scale. Neither by liberty did he ever mean license. So far as I can comprehend the true sense of the word "democracy," I have never found my idea more broadly developed than by him. It is far more practical than any thing ever taught by Jefferson, and throws into deep shadow the performances of most of his modern disciples. The alternative to which he was

21

driven was not without embarrassments, which he soon had occasion to feel. In allying himself with a party in which conservative views had more or less positive control, he could not fail to understand that his doctrines would sometimes inspire many of his associates with distrust, and some with absolute dislike, even though they might tolerate a union for the sake of the obvious advantage of his effective abilities. In point of fact, he soon became a representative of the younger, the ardent, and the liberal division, which favored a policy more in harmony with the nature of our institutions than suited the adherents to long established ideas. Yet these were not long in finding out that he was possessed of powers to direct the popular sense, which, on the whole, it was not expedient for them to neglect. Presently an occasion made him prominent in the State elections. The inconsistency, which he could not fail to expose, of the power of secret societies with popular institutions, as illustrated in the well-known story of the abduction and death of Morgan, made him, first, a member of the Senate of this State, and afterward raised him to be the Governor for two terms. In all this public service he is found boldly adhering to his broad views, even when they were so much in advance as actually to conflict with popular prejudices. He led so far that few could keep pace with him. Some even jeered, and many absolutely denounced him. The opposition was so stubborn, at last, that he decided to withdraw from the field. Yet the period soon arrived when the wisdom of his course came to be fully recognized, and the disputed points of his policy firmly established.

I very much fear lest in this analysis I may have much too seriously fatigued your attention. Yet, without it, I am convinced that I cannot illustrate the various phenomena of Mr. Seward's public life, or point out the difficulties through which he was perpetually working his way.

Now begins to be felt beneath our feet the first tremulous motion of what ultimately proved the great earthquake that shook the party organizations to pieces. I have already alluded to the first hidden overture made by General Jackson to the Government of Mexico, through the agency of Anthony Butler. Failing in this intrigue to get the territory desired by purchase, the next stroke was to endeavor to steal it by the indirect process of colonizing emigration. I have no time to dwell on the details of that nefarious transaction, which, partially checked by the prudent timidity of Martin Van Buren, revived with vigor under the pseudo*-presidency of

---

* This word is intended to signify a doubt whether the decision hastily made in this case by irresponsible persons was a just one. It is much to be regretted that the precise position of the Vice-President, in such an emergency, had not been determined by the Supreme Court. In at

John Tyler, and was ultimately consummated with the sanction of James K. Polk.

But this daring policy, however well covered at its outset, did not fail gradually to fix upon it the attention of numbers of the calmest and most moderate thinkers of the country least bound by the fetters of either political school. Taken in connection with the arbitrary spirit manifested by the efforts to suppress by popular violence the proceedings of a handful of enthusiasts, who only claimed their unquestionable right to express in public their objections to the whole system of slavery, whether at home or abroad, their eyes began to open to the realization of how far the action of the Government and people had drifted from the original principles with which it started. Very slowly at first, but steadily afterward, the public sentiment went on gathering sufficient force to make itself an object of attention to the leading men of the two parties. For some years, the ordinary discipline, so thoroughly established among our habits, continued to resist even the heaviest strain which the slave-holding alliance thought proper to place upon it. But the moment came when the assumption of the right absolutely to control the expression of the sense of

least one of the three contingencies provided by the Constitution, he could be only a temporary agent. It seems to me he should have been so regarded in all.

the people, in the form of respectful petition to their own representatives, proved a burden too heavy to bear. The cord then snapped, and from that date the disintegration of the old organization may be observed steadily hastening to its close.

The sentiment of Mr. Seward on the subject of slavery had been early expressed. Previously to graduating at college, he had passed six months in the State of Georgia, but he seems not to have been converted by his experience to any faith in the system. His first public demonstration was made in a Fourth-of-July oration, delivered at Auburn, when he was twenty-four years old. The passage is sufficiently striking, in view of our later history, to merit quotation here. Speaking of the Union: " Those, too," he says, "misapprehend either the true interest of the people of these States, or their intelligence, who believe or profess to believe that a separation will ever take place between the North and the South. The people of the North have been seldom suspected of a want of attachment to the Union, and those of the South have been much misrepresented by a few politicians of a stormy character, who have ever been unsupported by the people there. The North will not willingly give up the power they now have in the national councils, of gradually completing a work of which, whether united or separate, from proximity of territory, we shall ever be interested — the emancipation of slaves. And the South will never, in a moment of resentment, expose themselves to a war with the North while they have such a great domestic population of slaves ready to embrace any opportunity to assert their freedom, and inflict their revenge." In this passage, the deliberate claim of a power in the Federal Government to emancipate slaves by legislation is not less remarkable than the miscalculation of the force of the passions which led the South, in the end, to the very step that brought on the predicted consequences. Yet in his conclusion he proved a prophet. But he then could little have foreseen the share he was to have in controlling the final convulsion.

Mr. Seward terminated his career as a State politician with a very elaborate exposition of his views of policy, presented with great ability. It was wise in him to retreat, leaving such a legacy, for he thus escaped complications with local interests and rival jealousies, which render perseverance in purely local struggles such a thankless labor. It was this error which for a long time impaired the usefulness of another great statesman of New York, De Witt Clinton. From this date, Mr. Seward remained several years in private life, steadily pursuing his profession. The course of public affairs had not proved propitious to his party. The gleam of light shed by the success of General Harrison, in the presidential election, had turned to darkness by his death, and the consequent succession of John Tyler. Then followed the sharply-disputed election of 1844, when, for the first time, was taught to the manipulators of nominations a new precedent by which to regulate their policy. The lesson was this: That between a man of proved abilities, marked character, and long services, like Henry Clay, on the one side, and one comparatively unknown, with a brief, insignificant career, like James K. Polk, as candidates for the presidency, the majority of the people will prefer the one against whom the least can be said. I shall have to recur to this matter by-and-by in another form.

But there was another and still more significant lesson taught to politicians on this occasion: This was, that the party organizations founded upon a compromise, excluding the vital issue affecting the country, were about to meet with another shock. The final accomplishment of the scheme of enlarging the slave-holding region, by the acquisition of Texas, was well understood to be certain, in the event of the election of Mr. James K. Polk. On the other hand, the course likely to be taken, should Mr. Clay prove the victor, was left uncertain. A demand to know his sentiments was made so imperative that it was not deemed by him prudent to evade it. Yet, a rent in the party was almost sure to follow, whatever might be his conclusion. The result was a weak attempt, in a letter, to reconcile opinions which had become too discordant to permit of such treatment. Mr. Seward, though he faithfully adhered to the party, was too sagacious not to foresee the effect upon that portion of it with which he most sympathised at home. A defection of sixteen thousand voters in New York turned the scale, and Mr. Polk was elevated to power. This was the first considerable fissure made in the existing parties, and it inured to the benefit of the so-called Democracy. But their turn came around next time, when they were wrecked on the same rock. Such was the inevitable consequence of persevering in the maintenance of a division wholly superficial and evasive of the real and true issue — the permanence of the slave-holding supremacy.

The consequences of the election of Mr. Polk were very serious. Not only was the State of Texas introduced, but a war with Mexico followed, and a much larger acquisition of territory at the peace than had been originally contemplated. The engineer had been "hoist with his own petard." The success of the war had naturally brought into notice the military leaders who most contributed to it. The election of 1829 established another precedent for the guidance of parties, which had been confirmed by the experience of 1840. This was in effect that, as between a civilian and a soldier, both of them of

marked character, and of abilities proved by sufficient service, the people prefer the soldier. General
Taylor had very much distinguished himself by his
Mexican campaign, and the Whig party seized the
earliest opportunity of enlisting him in its ranks.
All the old statesmen were set aside, to press him
into the arena, and, under a military banner, once
more to overcome the Democrats, as had been done
with Harrison. But, unluckily for the harmony of
the movement, it came out that Taylor was a planter
holding many slaves, in one of the richest cotton-
producing States. The notion of setting up such a
candidate in connection with an anti-slavery policy
advocated by numbers of the party, seemed at first
blush too preposterous to be countenanced for a
moment. Yet it must be conceded that Mr. Seward
undertook the difficult task of advocating the inconsistency. I will frankly confess that I was one
among many of his friends in New England who
could not become reconciled to the contradiction
apparent in this proceeding. We had reluctantly
acquiesced in the ambiguous policy of Mr. Clay four
years before ; but when it came to this, that we were
called to give even a tacit ratification of the series
of revolting measures that followed, including the
Mexican war, and still more to elevate to the highest
post of the country, as a reward for his services, a
slave-holder having every possible inducement to

perpetuate the evil of which we complained, it proved a heavier load than we could bear. The consequence was a very considerable secession from the party, and an effort to bring before the public an independent nomination. This was carried out in what has ever since been remembered as the Buffalo Convention. Simultaneously with this movement, a similar one had been made in the Democratic party, a section of which of considerable force in New York, dissatisfied with the nomination of Lewis Cass, ultimately consented to make a part of the same assembly. The end was the nomination of Mr. Van Buren, and a declaration, for the first time, of a system of policy distinctly founded upon the true issues agitating the country.

But, however the fact may be in the details of ordinary life, it is quite certain that, in the conflicts of politics, the persons who try the hardest to press straight forward to their object not unfrequently find themselves landed at the end of the opposite road. The effect of the nomination of Mr. Van Buren was to make us, his opponents, contribute to the triumph of General Taylor, more decisively than if we had voted for him directly. This it was that proved the wisdom of Mr. Seward in holding back from our action.

Yet, with the success of General Taylor, the position in which Mr. Seward found himself seems to me, even now, to have been the most critical one in his life. He had in the canvass allowed himself to be freely used as an instrument to conciliate numbers of his friends, strongly tempted to secede. In order to retain them he had to hold fast to his own ground, and even to give assurance of his confidence that it would be ultimately sustained in case of victory. I have lately read with care such reports of his speeches during that canvass as I could find; and from that perusal I am constrained to admit that, much as I doubted his good faith at the time, I cannot perceive any failure in consistency or in committing himself to any policy which might follow, adverse to the expectations he held out. In other words, he kept himself free to influence it favorably if he could, or to disavow it if it should prove to be adverse. It was an honest, though not altogether a safe, position in case of success. General Taylor was made President, and simultaneously Mr. Seward was, for the first time, transferred from the field of State to that of National affairs. He came into the Senate of the United States, not to leave it for twelve years. He came under circumstances of no trifling embarrassment. The new President was at the time utterly unknown to the public men, and especially to him. He had been elected by a party still greatly divided in sentiment upon the grave questions about to come up for a decision. The chance of the pre-

ponderance of a policy favorable to freedom was by
no means flattering. An inexperienced President is
obliged to consume much of his early days in office
in correcting the mistakes he commits, before he
gets to an understanding with his advisers. I am
very sure that Mr. Seward felt for some time quite
uncertain what the issue would be. Every thing
depended upon the natural powers of General Taylor
to distinguish the true from the false path. Happily
for Mr. Seward, he determined to be guided by his
counsel.

A tract of territory had been acquired by the war
far more spacious than had been contemplated by
the originators of the policy, and now the question
came up whether all of the excess should be dedi-
cated to the use of freemen, or of masters and serv-
ants, as Texas had been. In other words, should
slavery be tolerated and extended indefinitely?
Early measures had been taken to pave the way for
it, by abrogating such portions of the existing Mexican law as might seem in conflict with it. But the
President determined to give no countenance to that
policy, and Mr. Seward was left at liberty to come
forward at once as an independent champion of
freedom.

It was a critical moment in the great struggle,
out of which the Government was to issue either as
an oligarchy, controlling all things in the interest of

a class, or else in a fuller development in harmony with the declared objects of its first construction. A remarkable number of men of superior abilities had been collected in the Senate just at this moment, all of whom had grown gray under the existing organization of parties, and were little disposed to favor innovations. Mr. Calhoun and Mr. Clay, though widely differing on other points, equally relucted at the agitation of slavery. Mr. Webster, on his part, never could make up his mind to meet it fully in the face. All manifested a desire to resort once more to some form of compromise, synonymous with a practical concession to the slave-holding pretensions. The immediate question was upon the admission of the newly-acquired Territory of California into the Union as a free State. The advocates of slavery insisted upon tacking to it conditions inuring to the support of their system in other respects, as a consideration proper to be granted for their acquiescence. In other words, it was another bargain to uphold slavery. And now, for the first time, Mr. Seward came forth on the great national arena to try his strength against his formidable competitors. Three successive speeches — one on the 11th of March, the next on the 2d of July, and the last on the 11th of September, of the year 1850 — displayed in the clearest light his whole policy on this vital subject. At the very outset he declared himself opposed to a compromise in any and all the forms in which it had been proposed; and he followed up the words with a close argument against each of those forms. He then went on boldly to grapple with the oft-repeated threats of disunion, as a consequence of emancipation, in a manner rarely heard before in that hall. Casting off the shackles of party discipline, he used these memorable words: "Here, then, is the point of my separation from both of these parties. I feel assured that slavery must give way, and will give way, to the salutary instructions of economy and to the ripening influences of humanity; that emancipation is inevitable, and IS NEAR; that it may be hastened or hindered; and, whether it shall be peaceful or violent, depends upon the question whether it be hastened or hindered: that all measures which fortify slavery or extend it tend to the consummation of violence; all that check its extension and abate its strength tend to its peaceful extirpation. But I will adopt none but lawful, constitutional, and peaceful means to secure even that end; *and none such can I or will I forego.*" Prophetic words, indeed, which it would have been well had they been properly heeded at the time by the besotted men who, ten years later, rushed upon their own ruin.

It was in this speech, also, that he enunciated the doctrine of a higher law than the Constitution, which gave rise to an infinite amount of outcry from even a very respectable class of people, who were shocked at the license thought to be implied by such an appeal. But it seems to me that no truth is more obvious than this, that all powers of government and legislation are closely restricted within a limitation beyond which they cannot pass without being stripped of their force. This limitation may be purely material, or it may be moral, but in either case its power is similar, if not the same.

It is a familiar story, which is told in the books, of Canute, the great Danish conqueror of Great Britain, that once, when his courtiers were vying with each other in magnifying their sense of his omnipotence, he simply ordered his chair to be approached to the advancing tide of the ocean, and loudly commanded the waves to retire. The flatterers understood the hint, and were abashed by this withering illustration of the " higher law."

In the declaration of his policy in these three speeches Mr. Seward was substantially supporting what had been agreed upon as within the line of the administration of General Taylor. And, so far as it was successfully carried out under his auspices, it must be admitted that it greatly contributed to remedy the evils anticipated from the slave-holding intrigues of twenty years. He was now, to all outward appearance, on the top wave of fortune, not unlikely to infuse into the national system a much more consistent system of principles than it had been its fortune to contain for many years. A single stroke from the higher law brought all his castle-building to the ground. A few days of illness, and the President was no more. To cite the words of an old poet :

> "Oh, frail estate of human things,
>   And slippery hopes below!
> Now, to our cost, your emptiness we know,
> Assurance here is never to be sought ;
> He toiled, he gained, but lived not to enjoy."

Scarcely could a blow be more overwhelming. The loss of the President was, in due course, supplied by the accession of the Vice-President, Mr. Fillmore. But with him came in the conservative section of the party, which had never reposed confidence in Mr. Seward. From that moment he was reduced once more to his old position as depending exclusively on his own powers, and had, as before, nothing to look for in official influence but opposition. The turn of things was decisive. The leading advocates of the policy of compromise freshened up to their labors, and the result was the adoption of a series of measures passing under that term, which the purblind authors fondly hoped would indefinitely postpone the earthquake, at the very moment rumbling under their feet. This memorable compact, entered into by three of the most eminent of our statesmen in the present century—Mr. Calhoun, Mr. Clay, and Mr. Webster—will forever remain as a proof of their own infatuation, and of nothing else. They might just as well have attempted to stop the torrent of Niagara with a drag-net.

One effect of this proceeding was soon made perceptible. It proved a death-blow to one of the party organizations. At the succeeding presidential election, the conservative section of the Whigs having failed in securing a nomination of a candidate to suit their views, rather than to vote for General Scott, understood to represent other sentiments, passed almost in mass over to the Democracy, and voted for Franklin Pierce. The result was, that the most insignificant and unworthy candidate ever yet presented to the suffrages of the people, in a contested election, was chosen by a greater majority than ever was given to the best.

From this moment the course of things rapidly assumed a more natural and consistent shape. The new Administration was soon found to be entirely under the control of the ultra slave-holders, and the policy of forcing slavery into the unoccupied regions of the West was unscrupulously pushed with their connivance. With these proceedings began the great reaction in the North and West. At last the election of 1856 displayed the fact that parties had thrown off disguises, and were placing themselves upon the real issues vital to the country. Although the result still favored the slave-holders, and James Buchanan was made to succeed Franklin Pierce, the severity of the struggle indicated but too plainly the beginning of the end. From this moment the Republican party became the true antagonist to that domination.

Mr. Seward now, for the first time, enjoyed the great advantage of being perfectly free from embarrassments springing out of a union with paralyzing associates in the same party. He took the field with all his vigor, and the speeches which he made, both in the Senate and before the people, remain to testify to his powers, and his success. The effects of the new union, reënforced by the extreme policy adopted by the opposite side, were made perceptible in the steady increase of the minorities in both Houses of Congress. The opening of the Thirty-sixth Congress showed that in the popular branch the Republican party counted a plurality of the members. After a long-continued struggle, they succeeded in electing their Speaker. It looked as if the handwriting would soon be visible on the wall.

Then came the moment when a candidate of the party, at last thoroughly organized, was to be nominated for the presidency of 1861. Mr. Seward, in his ten years of service in the Senate, had completely developed his capacity as a great leader in difficult times. With the singular mixture of boldness and moderation which distinguished him from all others, he had maintained his ground against all the assaults made upon him by the ablest of the slave-holding statesmen in their stronghold of the Senate. He had known how to pursue that narrow path between license in discussion on the one hand, and personal altercation on the other, which is so seldom faithfully adhered to by public men, especially when cunning fencers are ever lying in wait to entrap them. He had also enjoyed the benefit of experience in his administration while Governor of New York, which had made him familiar as well with executive as with legislative forms of business. The older men of great note had vanished, so as to make his party prominence more marked than ever. As a consequence, when the nominating convention assembled at Chicago, the eyes of all were turned toward him as the candidate, of all others, the most distinguished by the qualities that recommend people to high places. A large plurality had been chosen as delegates friendly to him, and the general expectation was that he would be nominated at once. But it was remembered that, in 1844, Henry Clay was defeated because he had a long record of public service, from which many marked sayings and doings might be quoted to affect impressible waverers, and James K. Polk was elected because nobody could quote any thing against him, for the reason that he had never said or done any thing worth quoting at all. Furthermore, the ghosts of the higher law and of the irrepressible conflict flitted about to alarm excited imaginations. Last but not least came in the element of bargain and management, manipulated by adepts at intrigue, which is almost inseparable from similar assemblies. The effect of all these influences united was to turn the tide at last, and Mr. Seward, the veteran champion of the reforming policy, was set aside in favor of a gentleman as little known by any thing he had ever done as the most sanguine friend of such a selection could desire. The fact is beyond contradiction that no person, ever before nominated with any reasonable probability of success, had had so little of public service to show for his reward.

Placing myself in the attitude of Mr. Seward, at the moment when the news of so strange a decision would reach his ears, I think I might, like *Amiens*, in the play, have moralized for an instant on man's ingratitude, and been warned by the example of Aristides, or even the worse fate of Barneveld and the two De Witts, not to press further in a career in which the strong were to be ostracized, because of their strength, and the weak were to be pushed into places of danger, on the score of their feebleness. To be elected for the reason that a person has never done any thing to display his powers of usefulness to bring about positive results, would seem to be like making elevation to power the prize of the greatest insignificance. Under such circumstances, a successful man might fairly infer that the selection of himself implied, on its face, rather an insult than a compliment.

But Mr. Seward, when he heard of it, did not reason on this low level. That he deeply felt such a refusal to recognize the value of his long and earnest labors in a perilous cause, I have every reason to believe. For it was precisely at this moment that the intimacy with which he sometime honored me dates its commencement. I had been long watching his course with the deepest interest, sometimes fearful lest he might bend toward the delusive track of expediency, at others impatient at his calmness in moments fit to call out the fire of Demosthenes, yet, on the whole, if I may be so bold as to confess it, fastened to his footsteps by the conviction that he alone, of all others, had most marked himself as a disciple of the school in which I had been bred myself. In this state of mind I had indulged a strong hope, not only that his splendid services would meet with a just acknowledgment, but that his future guidance might be depended on in the event of critical conjunctures.

I was at the time in the public service at Washington, and much cast down on hearing of the result. Mr. Seward had been at Auburn, and was just returned. I had not seen the answer to his friends, written from that place on the 31st of May, signifying his ready acquiescence in the result, and, if I had, I might not have put entire trust in it as a full expression of his inmost heart. The day after his return he called in his carriage at my door and asked me to get in and drive with him to the Capitol. He had never done this before, but I promptly accepted his offer. Full of disgust at the management contrived to defeat his nomination, I did not hesitate in expressing it to him in the most forcible terms. But I found no corresponding response. I saw that he had been grievously disappointed, and that he felt the blow so effectually aimed at him. But he gave no sound of discontent. On the contrary, he calmly deprecated all similar complaints, and at once turned my attention to the duty of heartily accepting the situation for the sake of the cause. The declaration of principles put forth by the convention was perfectly satisfactory, and it now became his friends to look only to the work of securing their establishment.

Such was the burden of the conversation for the greater part of the way. The tone was just the same as that in the public letter, while the language was more simple and unreserved. To me it was a revelation of the moral superiority of the man. I had heard so much in my time of the management attributed to New York politicians, from the days of Aaron Burr to those of Martin Van Buren, that I should not have been surprised to find him indulging in some details of the causes of his failure. But there was not a word. An experience like this drove me at once to the conclusion that, if such deportment as this passed under the denomination of management in New York, I should be glad to see its definition of magnanimity.

Neither were these merely brave words followed up by inaction or indifference. Mr. Seward entered into the canvass in behalf of his rival with the utmost energy. I was myself a witness and companion through a large part of his journey in the West. His speeches, made at almost every central point, indicate, not simply the fertility of his powers, but the fidelity with which he applied them to the purpose in hand. They still remain with us to testify for him themselves.

The election followed, making a new era in the history of this republic. The slave-holding power, which had governed for more than thirty years, had at last ceased to control. No sooner was the result known, than South Carolina lifted the banner of secession, not having chosen to wait for any assignable cause of grievance. Congress assembled at Washington to hold the last session under the administration of Mr. Buchanan. Tied hand and foot by the conditions under which he had received his nomination four years before, his course had been faltering and uncertain, meriting praise neither for prudence nor patriotism. A strong appeal, immediately put forth, to the sound sense and sterling principles of the honest, independent citizens of the country, without regard to party, backed up by an immediate preparation, quietly made, of the means at hand to maintain public order, in any contingency, might even then have put in check the tendency of multitudes to plunge into evil counsels. It does not appear that any thing of the kind was ever thought of. Treason had crept into the very heart of the cabinet, and a policy had been secretly at work to paralyze rather than to fortify the resources of the Executive. Every thing was drifting at the mercy of the winds and waves. One single hour of the will displayed by General Jackson, at the time when Mr. Calhoun, the most powerful leader secession ever had, was abetting active measures, would have stifled the fire in its cradle. But it was not to be. The evil came from the misfortune of a weak President in a perilous emergency.

Instead of taking this course, a message was sent to Congress by Mr. Buchanan, lamenting the fact of what he chose to call a secession of several States, but coupling with it a denial of any power to coerce them. This was in its essence an abandonment of all right to control popular resistance in that form. In the condition things were at that moment, with a cabinet divided, and both branches of the Legislature utterly without spirit to concert measures, the effect was equivalent to disintegration. Disaffection became rife everywhere south of Mason and Dixon's line. And, in the city of Washington itself, it became difficult to find, among the residents, persons wholly free from it. Rumors of some impending *coup d'état* vaguely floated in every breeze. From communications made to me by persons likely to know, I have every reason to think such projects were entertained by the class of more desperate adventurers. A plan of attacking the Constitution in its weakest part, the form of declaring the election of President in the month of February, had been gravely considered. Happily for the public peace, there was no leader at hand equal to the consummation of any such enterprise, so that more moderate counsels, based upon the not unreasonable confidence that victory was more sure by letting matters take their course, prevailed.

If such was the condition of the disaffected party, it was scarcely better with the loyal side. The President-elect was still at home in Illinois, giving

no signs of life, and there was no one of the faithful
men vested with authority to speak or act in his
behalf. That something ought to be done to keep
the control of the capital, and bridge over the interval before the 4th of March in peace and quiet, was
manifest. It was no time to go into consultations
that would inevitably lead to delays, if not to dissen-
sions. Neither was it wise to spread uneasiness and
alarm. In this emergency, I have it in my power to
speak only of what I know Mr. Seward effected on
his sole responsibility. Of his calmness in the
midst of difficulty, of his fertility in resource, of his
courage in at once breaking up the remnants of
party ties, and combining, as firmly as he could,
trusty men, whether in the cabinet, in the army, in
the municipal boards, or elsewhere, to secure the
object of keeping every thing steady, I had abun-
dant evidence. The hearty coöperation of General Scott, then Commander-in-Chief, although
surrounded by less than even lukewarm assistants,
proved of the highest value. The day is, perhaps,
not yet come, if it ever does, when all the details of
these operations will be disclosed. But, if it should,
it will only add one more to the many causes of
gratitude due by the country to the memory of Mr.
Seward.

But, out of all the sources of anxiety and distrust
heaped up in this most fearful interval, that which

appeared to many the most appalling was the fact that we were about to have, for our guide through this perilous strife, a person selected partly on account of the absence of positive qualities, so far as was known to the public, and absolutely without the advantage of any experience in national affairs, beyond the little that can be learned by an occupation for two years of a seat in the House of Representatives. The selection of Mr. Polk and Mr. Pierce, on the same principle, though in a less degree, for both of them had seen far more of service, had been, in a measure, justified to the country by their prompt recourse to the best-trained men of the party, as supports and guides, in the cabinet. But this was in times of profound internal quiet when the State machinery moved almost of itself; while, in this emergency, every wheel appeared clogged, and even the tenacity of the whole fabric was seriously tested. Neither was it any source of confidence to find that day passed after day, and not a syllable of intelligence came. It was clear, at least to me, that our chances of safety would rest upon an executive council composed of the wisest and most experienced men that could be found. So it seemed absolutely indispensable, on every account, that not only Mr. Seward should have been early secured in a prominent post, but that his advice, at least, should have been asked in regard to the completion of the organization. The value of such counsel in securing harmony in policy is too well understood to need explanation. But Mr. Lincoln as yet knew little of all this. His mind had not even opened to the nature of the crisis. From his secluded abode in the heart of Illinois, he was only taking the measure of geographical relations and party services, and beginning his operations where others commonly leave off, at the smaller end. Hence it was not until some time in the session that he disclosed his intention to place Mr. Seward in the most prominent place. So doubtful had some of Mr. Seward's friends been made, by this proceeding, of the spirit of the President, that they were disposed to advise him not to assume any responsibility under him. At least, this was the substance of what I understood him to say, when he was pleased to ask of me my sentiments. My answer was very short. No matter what the manner of the offer, his duty was to take the post. At the same time, it was quite clear to me that he stood in no need of my counsel. I should have mistaken his character if he had hesitated.

Let me not be understood as desiring to say a word in a spirit of derogation from the memory of Abraham Lincoln. He afterward proved himself before the world a pure, brave, capable and honest man, faithful to his arduous task, and laying down his life at the last as a penalty for his country's safety. At the same time, it is the duty of history, in dealing with all human action, to do strict justice in discriminating between persons, and by no means to award to one honors that clearly belong to another. I must, then, affirm without hesitation that, in the history of our Government down to this hour, no experiment so rash has ever been made as that of elevating to the head of affairs a man with so little previous preparation for his task as Mr. Lincoln. If this be true of him in regard to the course of domestic administration, with which he might be supposed partially familiar, it is eminently so in respect to the foreign relations, of which he knew absolutely nothing. Furthermore, he was quite deficient in his acquaintance with the character and qualities of public men, or their aptitude for the positions to which he assigned them. Indeed, he seldom selected them solely by that standard. Admitting this to be an accurate statement, the difficulties in the way of Mr. Seward on his assuming the duties of the foreign department may be readily imagined. The immediate reorganization of the service abroad was imperatively demanded at all points. The chief posts had been filled before that time with persons either lukewarm in the struggle or else positively sympathizing with the disaffected. One consequence had been the formation of impressions upon the representatives of foreign governments calculated in some measure to mislead their policy  Some were not unwilling to assume the question as already predetermined, and to prepare to accommodate themselves to the result of a divided sovereignty  Others were inclined only to watch the phenomena attending the dissolution, in order to adapt their policy to the variations, and take advantage of opportunities. Besides which, the failure of the greatest experiment of self-government ever made by a people was not without its effect upon every calculation of possibilities nearer home.  It may, then, be easily conceived what an effect could be produced in all quarters by the equivocal, half-hearted tone prevailing among the American agents themselves.

Yet, assuming it to be indispensable that the foreign service should be reorganized, a very grave difficulty forthwith presented itself.  The Republican party had been so generally in opposition that but few of its prominent members had had any advantages of experience in office.  And, in the foreign service especially, experience is almost indispensable to usefulness.  Mr. Seward himself came into the State Department with no acquaintance with the forms of business other than that obtained incidentally through his service in the Senate.  He had not had the benefit of official presence abroad, an advantage by no means trifling in conducting the foreign affairs. A still greater difficulty was that, within the range of selection to fill the respective posts abroad, hardly any person could be found better provided in this respect than himself. Moreover, the President, in distributing his places, did so with small reference to the qualifications in this particular line. It was either partisan service, or geographical position, or the length of the lists of names to commendatory papers, or the size of the salary, or the unblushing pertinacity of personal solicitation, that wrung from him many of his appointments. Yet, considering the nature of all these obstacles, it must be admitted that most of the neophytes acquitted themselves of their duty with far more of credit than could have been fairly expected from the commencement. I attribute this good fortune mainly to the sense of heavy responsibility stimulated by the peril of the country, and the admirable lead given by their chief. The marvelous fertility of his pen spread itself at once over every important point on the globe, and the lofty firmness of his tone infused a spirit of unity of action such as had never been witnessed before. The effect of this was that, from a state of utter demoralization at the outset, the foreign service rapidly became the most energetic and united organization thus far made abroad. The evidence of this will remain patent in the archives of the nation so long as they shall be suffered to endure.

It may be questioned whether any head of an executive department ever approached Mr. Seward in the extent and minuteness of the instructions he was constantly issuing during the critical period of the war. While necessarily subject to imperfection consequent upon the rapidity with which he wrote, his papers will occasion rather surprise at their general excellence than at any casual defects they may contain. Exception has been taken to his manner on some occasions as not in the best taste. And wiseacres have commented on his failure of sagacity in making over-confident predictions. But what was he to do in the face of all the nations of the earth? Was it to doubt, and qualify, and calculate probabilities? Would such a course have helped to win their confidence? I trow not. In the very darkest hour his clarion-voice rang out more sharp and clear in full faith of the triumph of the great cause than even in the moment of its complete success. And the consequence is, that the fame of William H. Seward as a sagacious statesman is more widely spread over every part of the globe than that of any other in our history.

But, great as were the services of Mr. Seward in his own peculiar department, it would be a mistake to infer that they were restricted within that limit.

I now come to a point where what appears to me to have been one of his greatest qualities, is to be set forth. It is impossible for two persons, in the relations of the President and the Secretary of State, to go on long together without taking a measure of their respective powers. Mr. Lincoln could not fail soon to perceive the fact that, whatever estimate he might put on his own acute judgment, he had to deal with a superior in native intellectual power, in extent of acquirement, in breadth of philosophical experience, and in the force of moral discipline. On the other hand, Mr. Seward could not have been long blind to the deficiencies of the chief in these respects, however highly he might value his integrity of purpose, his shrewd capacity, his vigorous ratiocination, and his generous and amiable disposition. The effect of these reciprocal discoveries could scarcely have been other than to undermine confidence, and to inspire suspicion in the weaker party of danger from the influence of the stronger. He might naturally become jealous of the imputation of being led, and fearful lest the labors of his secretary might be directed to his own aggrandizement at his expense. On the other hand, Mr. Seward might not find it difficult to penetrate the character of these speculations, and foresee their probable effect in abridging his powers of usefulness, and, perhaps, unsettling the very foundation of his position, should ambitious third parties scent the opportunities to edge him out.

Whether all that I have here described did or did not happen, I shall not be so bold as to say. But one thing I know, and this was, that, in order to cut up by the roots the possibility of misunderstanding from such causes, Mr. Seward deliberately came to the conclusion to stifle every sensation left in him of aspiration in the future, by establishing a distinct understanding with the President on that subject. The effect of this act of self-abnegation was soon apparent in the steady subsequent union of the parties. Thus it happened that Mr. Seward voluntarily dismissed forever the noblest dreams of an ambition he had the clearest right to indulge, in exchange for a more solid power to direct affairs for the benefit of the nation, through the name of another, who should yet appear in all later time to reap the honors due chiefly to his labors.

I am not going to touch upon the incidents of the great war. It is enough to say that Gettysburg and Vicksburg turned the tide; and the Administration had nothing more to fear from popular distrust. The election confirmed it in power, and little was left to do but to heal the wounds inflicted, and restore the blessed days of peace and prosperity. Scarcely had the necessary measures been matured, and Fortune begun once more to smile, when the hand of an assassin, unerring in its instinctive sagacity, vented all the rage of the baffled enemy upon the heads of the two individuals, of all others, who most distinctly symbolized the emancipation of the slave and the doom of the master's pride. Then followed a successor to the chair, sadly wanting in the happiest qualities of his predecessor, but readily moulded to the very same policy which had been inaugurated by him. In his earnestness to save it, Mr. Seward subordinated himself just as before. But the change of person proved little less disastrous to his hopes than it had been sixteen years before in the case of General Taylor. Nevertheless, he steadily and bravely adhered to the chief, for the sake of the policy, to the last, and quietly bore the odium of a failure he had no power to avert. It would have been worth all it cost, could he have succeeded. But, as it was, rarely has it been the fate of the same statesman to meet with two successive instances of such human vicissitudes.

In the spring of 1869 he bade a last farewell to public life. The veteran who had fought for years for the establishment of the great principles of liberty, clear of all hampering compromises, who bore on his front the gash received because he had worked too well — a scar which would have made a life-long political fortune for any purely military man — was permitted to repair in silence to his home, now

lonely from the loss of those who had made it his
delight, with fewer marks of recognition of his bril-
liant career than he would have had if he had been
the most insignificant of our Presidents. Such is one
more example of the fate that awaits "those who
hang on princes' favors," whether the sovereign be
one or be many. And now his native State, having
bestowed on him all the honors within her gift during
his life, with the natural pride in the career of so
great a son, has sought outside of her borders for
one of the humblest of his disciples to cull a few
fleeting flowers and spread them on his grave. While
I do honor to this manifestation on her part, I trust
I may be pardoned for remembering that he did not
save the State alone —

### HE SAVED THE NATION.

Let me turn from this subject to the more agree-
able task of pointing out to you some peculiar
qualities of Mr. Seward, which merit close attention
in any view taken of his character. Of these the
most marked was his indomitable courage. By
superficial observers among his contemporaries, the
breadth of his popular theory was set down as little
more than the agitation not unusual with most of
our ordinary demagogues. Hence the prejudices
more or less imbibed by many of his own party, and
others who knew nothing of him personally. Yet

the fact is indisputable that very few public men in our history can be cited who have shown so much indifference, in running directly counter to the popular passions when highly excited, as he did. And in such action it is clear that he could have been prompted by no motive other than the highest of personal duty.

Hitherto, I have treated only of his public life. I now propose to touch on his professional career, to which, though not attractive to him, he steadily adhered so long as it was practicable. Had he devoted himself to it exclusively, I have not a shadow of doubt he would have attained a position of the very first rank. I dwell on it now only in connection with a single case which will serve to illustrate as well his courage as his power. This is the case of the miserable negro William Freeman. The fact of his murdering at night all the members of a highly-respectable family in the neighborhood of Auburn, without any apparent motive, is too well remembered here to this day to need repeating the horrible details. It is sufficient to say that the passions of the people in all the country round about were fearfully but not unnaturally aroused. They demanded immediate justice with so much vehemence that, from fear of violence, extraordinary measures were resorted to by the State authorities to hasten the trial, in the very vicinity of the outrage. In the

State prison at Auburn it had so happened that, shortly before, a white convict had killed one of his associates. He had called upon Mr. Seward to defend him at his trial, and he had consented to appear. This act of his had not been viewed favorably in the neighborhood. But, when the crime of the negro was soon afterward divulged, the popular indignation rose to such a height that it was with much difficulty he could be conveyed in safety to the jail. So great was the rage, that nothing but the public declaration of one of the county judges, made on the spot, not only that he must certainly be executed, but also that "no Governor Seward would interpose to defend him," availed to shelter him from summary vengeance. Immediately afterward, the law partners of Mr. Seward assumed the responsibility of confirming that promise of the judge, without consulting him.

At that moment Mr. Seward had happily been absent from home. But, when he was expected to return, there was great anxiety among his friends and relatives, lest he should meet with insult, if not positive outrage, in his transit from the railway-station to his house. The excitement had scarcely abated when the two cases came up for trial. In the first, Mr. Seward endeavored to procure a postponement, but it was in vain. The popular feeling would not submit to it. With the utmost difficulty were persons found fitted to make a jury. The argument rested on the insanity of the prisoner. But it carried no weight. Within a month the convict was tried, condemned, and executed. In this instance Mr. Seward had performed his part in the regular course of professional service. But, when the offense of the wretched creature Freeman was about to be submitted to the consideration of the court, it immediately appeared that not a soul of the large crowd present entertained the smallest sympathy for him. He was told that he might have the assistance of counsel if he would ask for it. His answer indicated utter ignorance of the meaning of the words. Under such circumstances what was to be done to comply with forms of law? There was a solemn pause in that thronged assembly. At last the silence was broken by the judge, who, addressing the professional men before him, asked, in a hopeless tone,

"WILL *any one* DEFEND THIS MAN?"

And here again was a breathless pause, broken at last by a quiet movement of a solitary man, as he rose in his place, who, in the face of the eager crowd, briefly replied, "May it please the court, *I* appear as counsel for the prisoner."

This volunteer was WILLIAM HENRY SEWARD, the very man whom the excited multitude had already warned not to interpose to defend him.

I know not what others may think of this simple picture, but, in my humble view, it presents a scene of moral sublimity rarely to be met with in the paths of our ordinary life. At this juncture, had WILLIAM H. SEWARD been found anywhere at night alone, and unprotected by the powerful law-abiding habits of the region about him, his body would probably have been discovered in the morning hanging from the next tree. What motive could have impelled him to encounter so much indignation for this act? He had been not at all insensible to the pleasure of popularity in public life. Here he was not only injuring his own interests, but that of the party with which he was associated. In vain did it labor to disavow all connection or sympathy with him. The press on all sides thundered its denunciations over his head. The elections all went one way. The Democratic party came sweepingly into the ascendant. And all about the life of a negro idiot?

I think I do not exaggerate in expressing an humble opinion, that the argument in the defense is one of the most eloquent ever made in the language. I have no time to dwell on it, further than to quote a few passages assigning his reason for his conduct: " For William Freeman as a murderer, I have no commission to speak. If he had silver and gold accumulated, with the frugality of a Crœsus, and should pour it all at my feet, I would not stand an hour between him and his avenger. But for the innocent, it is my right — it is my duty — to speak. If this sea of blood was *innocently* shed, then it is my duty to stand beside him, until his steps lose their hold upon the scaffold. 'Thou shalt not kill' is a commandment, addressed not to him alone, but to me, to you, to the court, and to the whole community. There are no exceptions from that commandment, at least, in civil life, save those of self-defense, and capital punishment for crime in the due and just administration of the law. There is not only a question, then, whether the prisoner has shed the blood of his fellow-man, but the question whether we shall unlawfully shed his blood. I should be guilty of murder if, in my present relation, I saw the executioner waiting for an insane man, and failed to say or failed to do, in his behalf, all that my ability allowed."

And again he says: " I am arraigned before you for undue manifestations of zeal and excitement. My answer to all such charges shall be brief. When this cause shall have been committed to you, I shall be happy indeed if it shall appear that my only error has been that I felt too much, thought too intensely, or acted too faithfully."

But the significant and most eloquent passage is this: " I plead not for a murderer. I have no inducement, no motive to do so. I have addressed my fellow-citizens in many various relations, when rewards of wealth and fame awaited me. I have been cheered on other occasions by manifestations of popular approbation and sympathy; and, where there was no such encouragement, I had at least the gratitude of him whose cause I defended. But I speak now in the hearing of a people who have prejudged the prisoner, and condemned me for pleading in his behalf. He is a convict, a pauper, a negro, without intellect, sense, or emotion. My child, with an affectionate smile, disarms my care-worn face of its frown whenever I cross my threshold. The beggar in the street obliges me to give, because he says ' God bless you' as I pass. My dog caresses me with fondness if I will but smile on him. My horse recognizes me when I fill his manger. But what reward, what gratitude, what sympathy and affection can I expect here? There the prisoner sits; look at him. Look at the assemblage around you. Listen to their ill-suppressed censures and their excited fears, and tell me where among my neighbors or my fellow-men, where even in his heart can I expect to find the sentiment, the thought, not to say of reward or acknowledgment, but even of recognition. I sat here two weeks during the preliminary trial. I stood here between the prisoner and the jury nine hours, and pleaded for the wretch that he was insane, and he did not even know he was on trial. And when all was done, the jury thought — at least eleven of them thought — that I had been deceiving them, or was self-deceived. They read signs of intelligence in his idiotic smile, and of cunning and malice in his stolid insensibility. They rendered a verdict that 'he was sane enough to be tried' — a contemptible compromise verdict in a capital case — and then they looked, with what emotions God and they only know, upon his arraignment. The District Attorney, speaking in his adder-ear, bade him rise, and, reading to him one indictment, asked him whether he wanted a trial, and the poor fool answered 'No.' 'Have you counsel?' 'No.' And they went through the same mockery, the prisoner giving the same answers, until a third indictment was thundered in his ears, and he stood before the court silent, motionless, and bewildered. Gentlemen, you may think of this evidence, bring in what verdict you can, but I asseverate before Heaven and you that, to the best of my knowledge and belief, the prisoner at the bar does not at this moment know why it is that my shadow falls on you instead of his own. I speak with all sincerity and earnestness, not because I expect my opinion to have weight, but I would disarm the injurious impression that I am speaking merely as a lawyer speaks for his client. I am not the prisoner's lawyer. I am, indeed, a volunteer in his behalf.

But society and mankind have the deepest interests at stake. I am the lawyer for society, for mankind, shocked beyond the power of expression at the scene I have witnessed here, of trying a maniac as a malefactor."

There cannot be a doubt that, in this statement of his motives, Mr. Seward uttered nothing more than the simple truth. It was to rescue from violation the broad principle of morals, that guilt can only be measured by responsibility in the reciprocal relations of the human race. Yet, the jury brought in a verdict against the prisoner, and the judge pronounced the sentence of execution. Nothing daunted by all this, Mr. Seward persisted in interposing every possible dilatory measure, until the evidence of the condition of the man gradually forced itself so vividly upon the conviction of the very judge who had tried and condemned him, that, when officially called upon to go over the work once more, he declined it as impracticable. Mr. Seward was now clearly proved to have been right, so far as his action had gone before the law. But, when the time came for the end of Freeman by a natural death, seven physicians of the vicinity were summoned to a *post-mortem* examination of his brain, and the result at which they arrived was that it displayed indications of deep, chronic disease. Mr. Seward had been right from the start. He had upheld a broad general

principle at enormous personal hazard, and he never
received the smallest return for it, excepting in the
satisfaction to his own conscience of a work faithfully performed.

I pass from this illustration of the resolute will
and courage of the man, to another of a wholly different and still higher kind. I shall not weary your
patience by going over the well-known details of the
seizure by our gallant countryman, Admiral Wilkes,
of the two rebel emissaries, Mason and Slidell, by
forcibly taking them from a British passenger-
steamer, then on her way over the high seas to a
British port. You can all remember how much
delighted every body was with the news. Few
stopped to think of the possible consequences as
affecting the rights of neutral nations. Some erro-
neous precedents were published in the journals
which quieted possible doubts. Admiral Wilkes
immediately received the official approbation of the
House of Representatives and the Secretary of the
Navy, and rose in a moment to the height of a
popular hero. Crowded public meetings everywhere
joined in their acclamations, proudly exultant at the
gallant deed. On the other hand, the effect of
the violent proceeding, when divulged in Great
Britain, no one had a better opportunity to understand than I myself. It was at once presumed to
have been authorized by the Government, so that

no course was regarded as left to the ministry other than to demand immediate satisfaction for the insult. War was considered as inevitable; hence provision was promptly made by many to remove American property out of the risk of confiscation, The dock-yards resounded by night as well as by day with the ring of the hammers, fitting out the largest iron-clads, and orders went forth to assemble the most available troops for immediate embarkation to the points in America closest upon our northern border. A cabinet council was promptly assembled. Four dispatches were drawn up on the same day, the 30th of November, three of them addressed to the British minister at Washington, Lord Lyons, and one to the Lords Commissioners of the Admiralty. All of them distinctly anticipated an immediate rupture, and made provision for the event. One of these, very carefully prepared, instructed Lord Lyons to protest against the offensive act, and, in case the Secretary of State should not voluntarily offer redress by a delivery of the men, to make a demand of their restoration. The second directed Lord Lyons to permit of no delay of an affirmative answer beyond seven days. Should no such answer appear within that time, his lordship was formally instructed to withdraw with all his legation and all the archives of the legation, and to make the best of his way to London. The fourth letter, addressed to the Admiralty, contained instructions to prepare all the naval officers stationed in America for the breaking out of hostilities.

Looking at these proceedings as calmly as I can from our present point of view, it seems impossible for me to doubt that the issue of this peremptory demand had been already prejudged by her Majesty's ministers. They did not themselves believe that the men would be restored. Hence what seems to me the needless offensiveness of these preliminaries prompted, no doubt, by the violence of the popular feeling, which would insist upon an immediate display of what would be called a "proper spirit." Yet, had it been judged possible to await for a few days the reception of official intelligence, then on its way from Washington, these gentlemen would have learned from Mr. Seward that they were precipitate in their action at least, and wholly without a basis in presuming evil intentions. Moreover, they would have had the assurance that the act was without authority; and that the Government was ready to listen to any reasonable representation that might be forthcoming. It thus appears that her Majesty's Government had placed themselves at the outset in a false position, needlessly offensive, and only provocative of war without a cause. For the peremptory nature of the overture, however clothed in moderate terms, merely complicated the difficulty of responding in any tone that would at all quiet the excited temper of the American people.

It was the writing of that preliminary dispatch that saved the dignity of the country. Mr. Seward could point to it to prove that his action, when finally taken, had not been prompted by intimidation. The precipitate British course had betrayed the rudeness of distrust, and nothing more. He had been ready to hear and discuss the question impartially, and solely on its merits. But the people of the United States had thought of none of these things. They were satisfied with the fancied glory of the deed, and very far from disposed to sanction the smallest recantation. As to the demand for the surrender of the men, the thing was not to be thought of. They must be retained at any hazard. Such was the universal sense, and it is this which generally controls the actions of those who hold office in a popular government. Yet the fact was to me clear from the first that the act was not justifiable. Many of the most enlightened neutral nations had signified as much in a friendly way, and had wished to open to us some easy method of retreat. A war with Great Britain to maintain an unsound principle, merely because the people made a hero of Admiral Wilkes, would probably have ended in a triumph of the rebellion and a permanent disruption of the Union, furnishing ever after a new example with which "to point a moral and adorn a tale." When the time came for the assembly of the cabinet to decide upon an answer to Great Britain, not a sign had been given by the President or any of the members favorable to concession. Mr. Seward, who had been charged with the official duty of furnishing the expected answer, assumed the responsibility of preparing his able argument upon which a decision was predicated to surrender the men. Upon him would have rested the whole weight of the popular indignation had it proved formidable. If I have been rightly informed, when read, it met with but few comments and less approbation. On the other hand, there was no resistance. Silence gave consent. It was the act of Mr. Seward, and his name was to be chiefly associated with it, whether for good or for evil. That name will ever stand signed at the foot of the dispatch. In my firm belief, that act saved the unity of the nation. It was like the fable of the Roman Curtius, who leaped into the abyss which could have been closed in no other way. The people acquiesced rather than approved, and to this day they have never manifested any sign of gratitude whatever.

In 1869 Mr. Seward returned home to Auburn, the wreck of his former self. The continuous con-

flicts of twenty years, and especially those of the
last eight, with the assassin's knife, had told heavily
on his frame. That home, too, was no longer what
it had been, when the gifted partner of his life and
a beloved daughter spread over it sunshine and joy,·
in peaceful times. Worst of all, the symptoms of a
subtle disease, creeping slowly from the extremities,
came to warn him that repose would be synonymous with decay. Nothing daunted, he determined
to fight the enemy to the last. He undertook the
laborious task of a journey around the globe.
What he modestly and yet sadly says of it himself
is found in the reply he made to the welcome given
him by his neighbors and friends on his return : " I
have had a long journey, which, in its inception,
seemed to many to be eccentric, but I trust that all
my neighbors and friends are now satisfied that it
was reasonable. I found that, in returning home
to the occupations which were before me, I was
expected to enjoy rest from labors and cares which
were thought to have been oppressive and severe.
I found, that, at my age, and in my condition of
health, 'rest was rust,' and nothing remained to
prevent rust but to keep in motion. I selected the
way that would do the least harm, give the least
offense, enable me to acquire the most knowledge,
and increase the power, if any remained, to do
good." The volume from which I quote, contain-

ing a very interesting account of the travels of Mr. Seward, has been issued to the world since his decease. The turn of his mind, ever indulging in wide speculation upon the objects presented to his observation, is as clearly marked in this as it is in any of his earlier productions. Hence it is clear that, however impaired may have been his tenement of clay, the living principle within held out firmly to the last. This book likewise shows, though expressed in very modest language, that the fame of the great statesman had reached the remotest and most exclusive nations of the Eastern Hemisphere, and had won for him — a simple private citizen — spontaneous recognitions such as heretofore, in those communities, have been extorted only by representatives of those sovereignties which they fear.

And now the chief part of my work is done. I have tried to test the statesman by the highest standard known to mankind. His career covers the whole of what I designate as the second period of our history — that, pending which, the heaviest clog to freedom, a perilous legacy from our forefathers, was, after long and severe conflict, at last happily removed. In this trial Mr. Seward played a great part. His mind, taking in the broadest view of practical popular government, never failed him in the useful application of his powers to the removal of all adventitious obstructions to its development. He was never a mere theorist or dreamer of possibilities he could not reach. He speculated boldly, but he was an actor all the while, and effected results. It is in this sense that I think my narrative has established for him a just claim to the high position I assigned to him at my outset. He may not, indeed, rise to the full stature of the philosopher-statesman, "equal to the present, reaching forward to the future," never seen even in the palmy days of ancient Greece, or perhaps anywhere else, but at least he stands in the first rank of those admitted most nearly to approach it.

But thus far I have considered him exclusively in his public life. The picture would scarcely seem complete, if I omitted a word about him as a man like all the rest of us. By nature he can scarcely be said to have been gifted with the advantage of an imposing presence, such as fell to the lot of Mr. Calhoun and Mr. Webster. Neither in face nor in figure would he have attracted particular notice, and both his voice and power of articulation were little favorable to the power of his elocution. Yet he had in a remarkable degree the faculty of fixing the hearer's attention — the surest test of oratorical superiority. His familiar conversation rarely kept in the dreary round of common-place, and often struck into original and instructive paths. His personal address was easy and careless, sometimes rather blunt. It lacked something of the polish of the most refined society, but there was a simplicity and heartiness in his genial hours that often brought one close to him in a moment. At times, when in good spirits, there seemed a superabundant glee, which spent itself in laughter springing from his own thoughts, more robust than could be wholly accounted for by any thing expressed. And yet it had a sympathetic power over the hearers almost irresistible. In his domestic relations he was pure and affectionate — ready to heed the monitions of a gifted and refined partner, and profit by her prudent counsel. Unhappily, her infirm health, breeding a strong inclination for retirement from the bustle and excitement of the society of Washington, materially detracted from the influence, as well as the satisfaction, attending her husband's elevated position. Our forefathers would marvel could they imagine it possible for me to claim credit for Mr. Seward on the score of his honesty as a public man. Yet the time has come when we must honor one who never bought nor sold a vote or a place, and who never permitted his public action to be contaminated in the atmosphere of corporation influence. On that subject I had occasion to know his sentiments more than once. Above all, he was earnestly impressed with religious feeling, never making parade of it, but never omitting every proper occasion to make it suitably respected. One of his finest traits was the calmness with which he endured all the various political assaults made upon him by opponents, and often by those of his own side. Few persons of his time encountered more. It is the nature of power always to raise a body of resistance in a relative proportion to the force of its own movement. Then came also the day of complaints raised by the large class fated to be aggrieved by disappointed hopes or imagined offenses, the arrogant, the incompetent, the rapacious, the treacherous, and the unscrupulous, always to be found intrenched around every fountain of political favors. Mr. Seward was never tempted to elevate the position of such persons by controversy, or to profit by opportunities for merited retribution, even when clearly within his grasp. To his intimate friends he was deeply attached. One of these who survives him — may I say his fidus Achates —

" It comes et *paribus curis* vestigia figit,"

whose singularly disinterested labor it has been to effect the elevation of others to power, and never his own, and to whose remarkable address I strongly suspect Mr. Seward owed many obligations of that kind, has been kind enough to submit to my perusal numbers of his confidential letters, received during interesting periods in the writer's life, which have been collected and bound in volumes. I have closely examined them, as laying bare the most secret impulses of his mind and heart. Yet, highly confidential as they appear on their face to be, I could not detect a single passage which, for his sake, "I could wish to blot."

The line of great statesmen in America may or may not stretch out,

"In yon bright track that fires the western skies,"

to the crack of doom. But the memory of him who guided our course, through the most appalling tempest yet experienced in our annals, can scarcely fail to confront all future aspirants in the same honorable career, as an example which every one of them may imitate to his advantage, but which few can hope to be so fortunate as to excel.

*QUARTETTE.* — " Integer Vitæ,"   -  -  -    *Fleming.*

*BLESSING.* — By Rev. Bishop COXE.

ORGAN DISMISSION.

Subsequent to the address the following resolutions, offered by Senator PERRY, were unanimously adopted by the Senate and concurred in by the Assembly :

*Resolved,* That the thanks of the Legislature of the State of New York be tendered to the Hon. CHARLES FRANCIS ADAMS, for the eloquent eulogium on the life, character and services of ex-Governor WILLIAM H. SEWARD, delivered at the request of the Legislature, on the 18th day of April, inst., and that a copy of the address be requested for publication.

*Resolved,* That a copy of these resolutions be forwarded to Mr. ADAMS, signed by the presiding officers and clerks of the Senate and Assembly.

An engrossed copy of the above resolutions, duly authenticated, was subsequently forwarded to Mr. ADAMS by the joint committee, accompanied by the following letter :

LETTER TO MR. ADAMS.

"STATE OF NEW YORK :
" SENATE CHAMBER,
" ALBANY, *May* 12, 1873. }

" Hon. CHARLES FRANCIS ADAMS :

" *Dear Sir* — Herewith I have the honor to inclose the joint resolutions of thanks to yourself, adopted by the Senate and Assembly on the 29th ult. In addition, I beg leave, on behalf of the joint committee, to express to you their sincere acknowledgments for your kind acceptance of their invitation, and for the very complete and eloquent address delivered on the occasion.

"You will observe that one of the resolutions contains a request that a copy of the address be furnished for publication. Entertaining the hope that you may be pleased to comply with this request, I have the honor to remain,

Gratefully yours,

"JOHN C. PERRY,

"*Chairman of Joint Committee.*"

The receipt of these resolutions was acknowledged by Mr. ADAMS as follows:

### Mr. Adams' Reply.

"QUINCY, *May* 14, 1873.

"Hon. J. C. PERRY, *etc., etc.:*

"*Dear Sir* — I have to acknowledge the reception of your letter of the 12th instant, and of the joint resolutions of the Senate and Assembly therein referred to.

"I pray you to accept, in their behalf, my grateful thanks for the manner in which they have honored me.

"In compliance with their request, I beg permission to transmit to you herewith a copy of the address revised for publication.

"I have the honor to be,

"Your obdt. servt.,

"C. F. ADAMS."